BIG CATS

By Steve Parker
Illustrated by Ian Jackson

BYEWAY BOOKS

First published in 2002 by
Miles Kelly Publishing Ltd
Bardfield Centre
Great Bardfield
Essex, CM7 4SL

This 2005 edition published by Byeway Books
Byeway Books Inc.
Lenexa, KS 66219, 866-4BYEWAY
www.byewaybooks.com

Editorial Director: Belinda Gallagher
Art Director: Clare Sleven
Assistant Editors: Nicola Jessop, Nicola Sail
Designer: Herring Bone Design
Artwork Commissioner: Lesley Cartlidge
Indexer: Jane Parker

Library of Congress Cataloging-in-Publication
Data is on file at the Library of Congress.

ISBN 1-933581-21-2

Printed in China

2 4 6 8 10 9 7 5 3 1

Contents

Tigers are biggest

Cat facts

- The Siberian tiger measures 11.5 ft (3.5 m) long, from nose to tail tip.
- It weighs up to 660 lb (300 kg)—as much as five adult people.

The **SIBERIAN TIGER** is not just a big cat—it's the biggest cat! This huge hunter prowls the cold, snowy lands of Eastern Asia. It is the rarest kind of tiger, too, with less than 200 left in the wild. The Bengal tiger of the Indian region is more common, with about 5,000 living wild.

The tiger has long fur on its cheeks, making its face look wide.

The Siberian tiger has thick fur to keep it warm in the ice and snow of winter.

Tigers have black stripes on their yellow, orange, or gold fur. The Siberian tiger has more white in its coat to help it blend in with its snowy landscape.

Man eaters!

Very rarely, tigers attack and eat people. These tigers are usually old or injured. They can't catch their normal prey such as deer, wild cattle, and wild pigs.

The Siberian tiger is heavily built. Its body hangs close to the ground.

2 Pumas make good mothers

Cat facts

- The puma has a nose-to-tail length of 7.3 ft (2.2 m).
- It lives in western North America and South America.

Like all big cats, the female **PUMA** is a very caring mother. She protects her babies, feeds them on her milk—and keeps them warm and safe in a den.

Baby big cats are called cubs. Puma cubs have spotty coats when they are first born. These fade as they get older.

Puma cubs feed on their mother's milk for about seven weeks. Then they begin to eat pieces of meat that their mother brings back to the den.

The mother cat licks her babies clean. She often moves them to a new den for extra safety.

Useful tails

Like the puma, the domestic cat has a long tail. This helps it to balance as it walks along narrow surfaces, and as it runs.

A mother puma usually has two or three cubs, but there may be as many as six!

Lions live in groups

Cat facts

- The male lion is 10 ft (3 m) long and weighs 440 lb (200 kg).
- The female lion is 8 ft (2.5 m) long and weighs 285 lb (130 kg).

LIONS are the only kind of cat that live together in a group. All other cats live alone (except for a mother with her babies). A group of lions is called a pride. There are usually between five and ten lions in a pride. They are mostly mothers with their young, and one or two males. Most lions live in Africa, with just a few hundred in India.

In a pride, the chief male lion is the father of all the cubs. His main job is to chase away other lions, so that they cannot steal prey from the pride's area.

The lion is the only big cat where the female and male look different. The male is bigger and has long, shaggy neck fur called a mane.

Padded paws

Lions have thick, leathery pads on the underside of their paws. These help the lion to move quietly and get a good grip on slippery rocks.

Male and female lions roar loudly. This frightens off other lions that aren't in their pride.

Jaguars love water

Cat facts

- The jaguar grows up to 8 ft (2.5 m) long, including its tail.
- It is a heavily built cat and weighs up to 330 lb (150 kg).
- Jaguars live in Central and South America.

Many cats hate water and getting wet. The **JAGUAR** loves it! This big cat is sturdy and strong, with large, powerful muscles. It likes to hunt around rivers, lakes, and swamps, and it can swim well. The jaguar catches water creatures such as turtles, caimans (types of crocodiles), crayfish, and snakes. It even dives under the surface to chase fish!

After a swim, the jaguar cleans and combs its fur, using its rough tongue and its sharp claws.

American cat!

The jaguar is the biggest cat in the Americas. With its spotty coat, it is similar to the leopard of Africa and Asia.

Each "spot" on the jaguar's coat is like a ring with a dark center. The patchy pattern helps the jaguar to blend in with leaves and twigs.

The jaguar creeps slowly through water without a splash or a ripple. It surprises prey such as deer and tapirs.

Caracals can leap

Cat facts

- The caracal is about 3 ft (90 cm) long, including its tail.
- It lives in Africa and the Middle East.

All cats can jump well. But one of the best leapers, for its body size, is the **CARACAL**. It is not a very big cat, yet it can spring forward more than 13 ft (4 m) in one bound. It can even jump 10 ft (3 m) in one leap—straight upwards!

The caracal is also called the desert lynx, because it likes dry areas—and because its ears have long tufts of fur like a real lynx.

The caracal eats rats, hares, birds, and baby animals such as antelopes and wild pigs. It also eats lizards and snakes.

The caracal lives in dry places such as rocky hills, grassland, scrub, and around the edges of deserts. Its gold color makes it difficult to spot among the brown plants and sandy soil.

Champion leap!

The caracal can jump four times its own body length. See how far you can jump—as if you are practicing for the long jump!

The caracal crouches down and then springs forward using its powerful rear legs.

6 The lynx likes snow

Cat facts

• The lynx is about 4 ft (1.2 m) long, including its short tail.

• Various kinds of lynx live in the north of Europe, Asia, and North America.

The **LYNX** is at home in the snow and ice of the far north. It has very thick fur to keep it warm. Even the tips of its ears have furry tufts. Its paws are large and wide, and they have fur underneath, too. The paws work like snowshoes, to prevent the lynx sinking into soft snow, or sliding on slippery ice.

The lynx has a very short tail, less than 8 in (20 cm) in length. A long tail might get so cold in the freezing winter, that it could suffer from frostbite.

Like many cats, the lynx searches for prey that are old, young, sick, or injured. These are easier to catch than strong, healthy prey!

Snow paws!

Press your fingers into flour, which is soft and white, like snow. Now put a bag over your hand. See how your "snow paw" sinks in less.

The lynx hunts deer, wild sheep and goats, hares, and birds. It may bury spare food in the snow and come back to eat it later.

The lynx's paws are wide and furry. They give a good grip on snow, ice, wet rocks, and slippery tree branches.

Snow leopards have sharp claws

Cat facts

- The snow leopard lives in the high mountains of central Asia.
- It measures 6.6 ft (2 m) long from nose to tail tip.

The **SNOW LEOPARD**, like other big cats, has five toes on each front foot and four toes on each back foot. Every toe has a sharp claw! The claws grip trees and rocks when climbing, and they slash and slice prey when hunting.

The snow leopard also uses its claws to comb its fur and scratch its skin.

The rare and beautiful snow leopard hunts in mountain forests and crags. It catches wild goats, sheep, birds, monkeys, and squirrels.

Smallest cat

The smallest kind of big cat is the clouded leopard of Southeast Asia. It lives almost all of its life in trees.

Like other cats, the snow leopard usually keeps its claws retracted. This means they are pulled back inside its pads, which are like pockets at the ends of its toes. This keeps the claws clean and sharp.

17

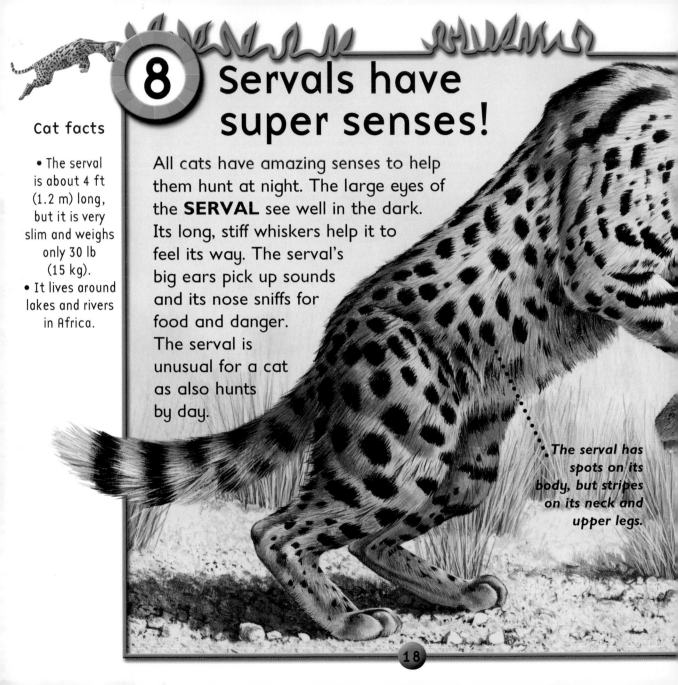

8 # Servals have super senses!

Cat facts

• The serval is about 4 ft (1.2 m) long, but it is very slim and weighs only 30 lb (15 kg).

• It lives around lakes and rivers in Africa.

All cats have amazing senses to help them hunt at night. The large eyes of the **SERVAL** see well in the dark. Its long, stiff whiskers help it to feel its way. The serval's big ears pick up sounds and its nose sniffs for food and danger. The serval is unusual for a cat as also hunts by day.

The serval has spots on its body, but stripes on its neck and upper legs.

Cat's eyes!

Cat's eyes have a shiny lining inside them. Some faint light bounces off this lining and makes the eyes glow in the dark.

As the serval pounces, it puts out its claws to hold down the victim. Then it bites with its long, sharp teeth to kill the prey.

The serval has long, slim legs. It peers through the reeds and rushes at the edge of a lake or river, races after its prey—then it pounces!

The serval's favorite meals include swamp rats, water voles, and baby ducks.

Leopards have a larder

Cat facts
• The leopard lives in many regions across Africa and southern Asia.
• It is about 8 ft (2.4 m) in total length.

Sometimes a cat like the **LEOPARD** catches prey which is too big to eat in one meal. So the leopard stores the leftovers up in a tree. Here they are kept safe from hungry hyenas and jackals too!

Leopards live in lots of places, from dry grassland and scrub to mountains, forests, and swamps. They even live around villages.

The leopard may wait on a branch, and then pounce silently on a victim below.

Every leopard has a different pattern of spots—just as every person has different fingerprints.

Black leopard!

The black panther is not a different kind of big cat. It's a leopard with very dark fur.

The leopard's favorite tree has scratch marks in the bark. They warn other leopards to keep away.

The leopard is strong enough to drag a whole gazelle up into a tree.

A leopard can catch large animals such as antelopes, which are three times its own size. When food is scarce, it will eat rats, mice, birds' eggs, and even insects such as beetles!

The speedy cheetah

Cat facts

• The cheetah measures about 6 ft (1.8 m) from nose to tail.

• It lives in Africa and western Asia.

No animal can run as fast as the **CHEETAH**. This big cat races along at 60 mph (100 km/h)—about as fast as a car on a highway. The cheetah can only keep up this speed for half a minute. Then it must stop to cool down and get its breath back.

Cheetahs hunt small gazelles, antelopes, hares, and other fast-running animals.

The cheetah tries to trip or knock over its victim, then pounces on it.

Cheetahs and many other kinds of big cat have become rare. Once, cats were killed for their fur, to make coats and hats. Today, all cats need our help to survive.

The cheetah likes dry, open places such as grassland and scrub. It cannot run very fast in thick woods!

Claws out!

The cheetah is the only cat that cannot pull its claws into its toes. The claws are big and blunt, like a dog's.

The cheetah has a small head, a slim and bendy body, and very long legs.

Index